W9-BVS-253
ordinary terrible things
ordinary terrible things
DISCARD

Forever and Ever
Dearly Beloved
Death Is Stupid
written and illustrated by Anastasia Higginbotham
THE FEMINIST PRESS
AT THE CITY UNIVERSITY OF NEW YORK
NEW YORK CITY

Published in 2016 by the Feminist Press
at the City University of New York
The Graduate Center
365 Fifth Avenue, Suite 5406
New York, NY 10016

feministpress.org

Copyright © 2016 by Anastasia Higginbotham

All rights reserved.

No part of this book may be reproduced, used, or stored in any information retrieval system or transmitted in any form or by any means, electronic, mechanical, photocopying, recording, or otherwise, without prior written permission from the Feminist Press at the City University of New York, except in the case of brief quotations embodied in critical articles and reviews.

First printing April 2016

Illustration and design by Anastasia Higginbotham
Photography by Alexa Hoyer
Production by Drew Stevens and Suki Boynton

Special thanks to Lionel Luongo Higginbotham for his careful editing and guidance.

Library of Congress Cataloging-in-Publication Data is available for this title.

Manufactured by Thomson-Shore, Dexter, MI, USA; RMA95HS74, December, 2015

R0445710466

# When a loved one dies

I know exactly how you feel.

people can say some...

Don't cry.
Just be grateful for the time you had with her.
... stupid things.

Even the people who care
about you most
may not know
what to say.

We lost her.
Then find her.
We can't, honey. She's gone.
Gone WHERE ?? Is she ever coming back?

Every life comes to an end.

She's in a
better place.

Dying is not a punishment.

Would I be in a better place if I died ?!!

Heavens NO!
But it mostly doesn't feel fair.

Death is NOT better. It's stupid.

We just mean she's at peace.
She can rest.
And don't say stupid.
Why can't she rest HERE with me and still be alive?

Here's your breakfast, Gramma. I'm going out to take care of your garden. If you need me for anything, just yell out the window. I'll come running!

Oh, thank you for letting me rest, dear. Now I don't have to die.

Some people may try to help and make it worse.
Now your gramma can watch over you wherever you are!

(whipped cream) →

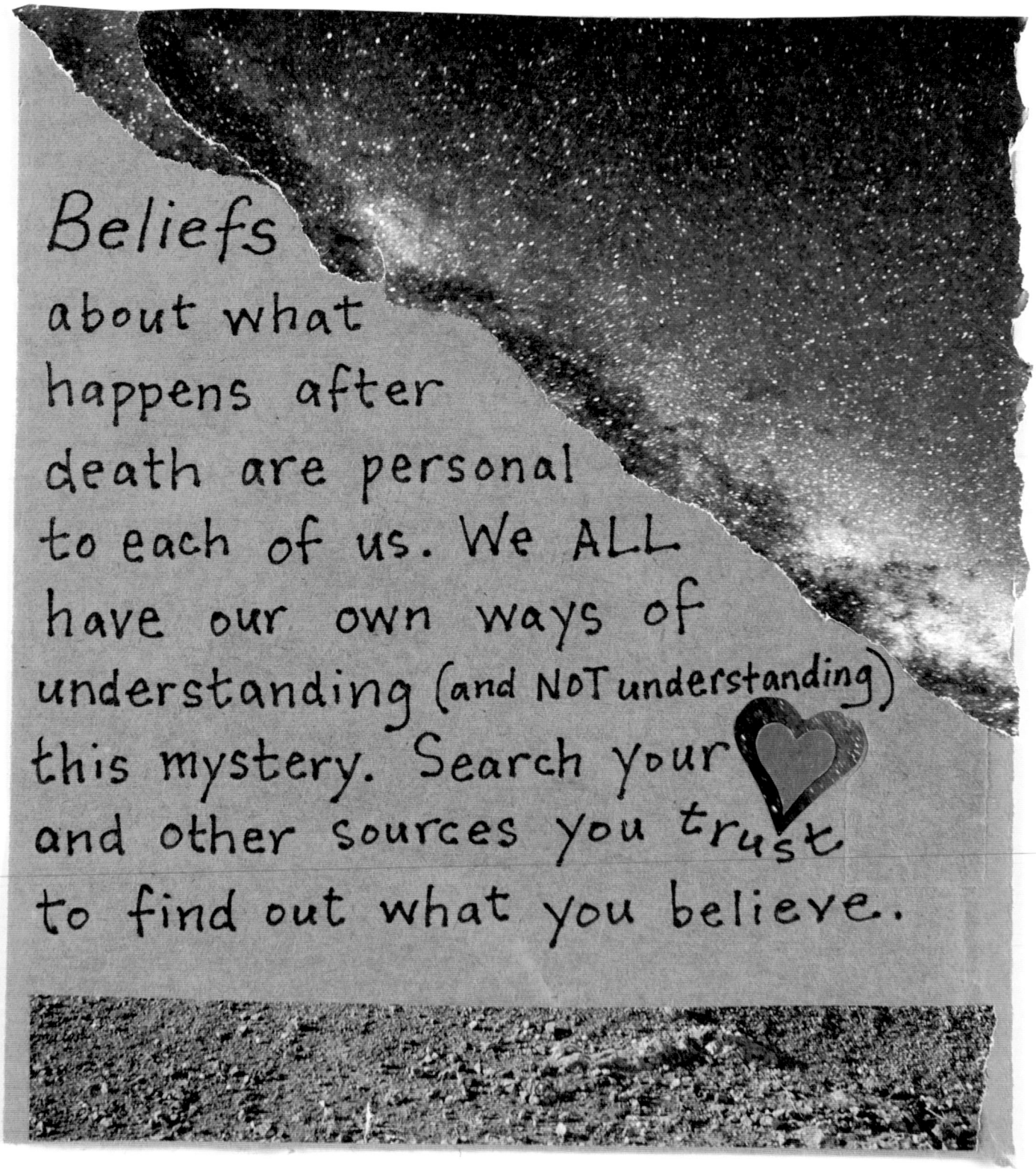
Beliefs
about what
happens after
death are personal
to each of us. We ALL
have our own ways of
understanding (and NOT understanding)
this mystery. Search your
and other sources you trust
to find out what you believe.

But beware of the lies.
She's only sleeping.

Don't say that to me.
Sleep is what I do and I wake up every morning.

Come on, honey. Time to go home.
My gramma isn't asleep. She died.

It takes courage to go on living...

Beautiful day!
...when
the one you
love has
died,

and to
accept that
death
cannot be
changed.

Everyone eventually has an experience of someone who died.

a member of their family

a good friend

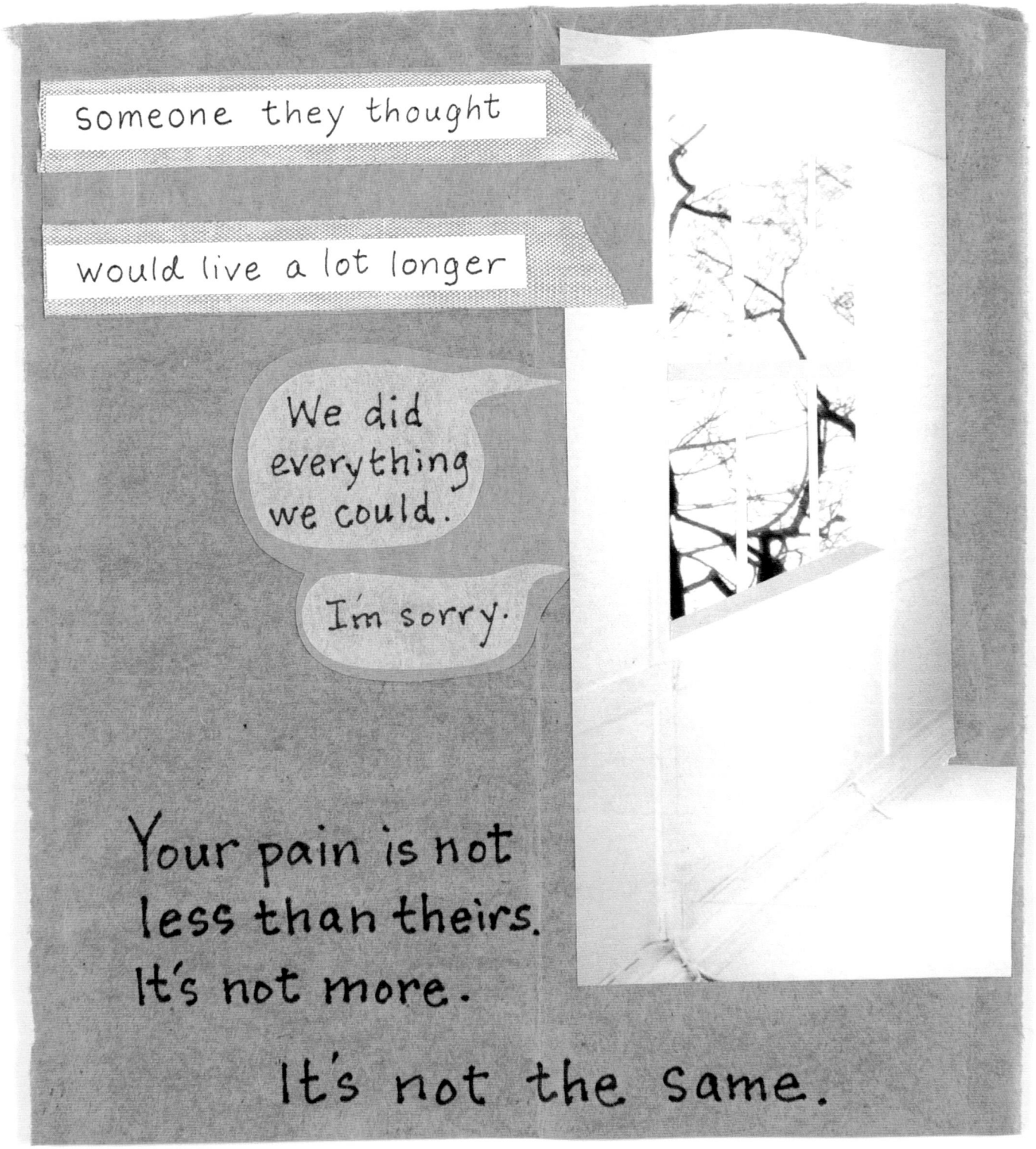
someone they thought
would live a lot longer
We did everything we could.
I'm sorry.
Your pain is not less than theirs. It's not more.
It's not the same.

Can I play in my room now?
Be sure to hang up that suit when you take it off!

I will.

You might
be
freaked
out

by the grief of those you depend on.
My dad cried at the funeral. Not the quiet kind of crying— it was the kind you can hear.

aahoooooo hoo
cough cough ahoooo
ahh hoo
hoo hooooo

My mom says to talk to Gramma in my imagination. I know what I would say.

Gramma, you shouldn't have died. I still need you.
Oh, honey, I know. Death is so stupid.

GRAMMA!!
You said stupid!!
Well, it is!! hee hee

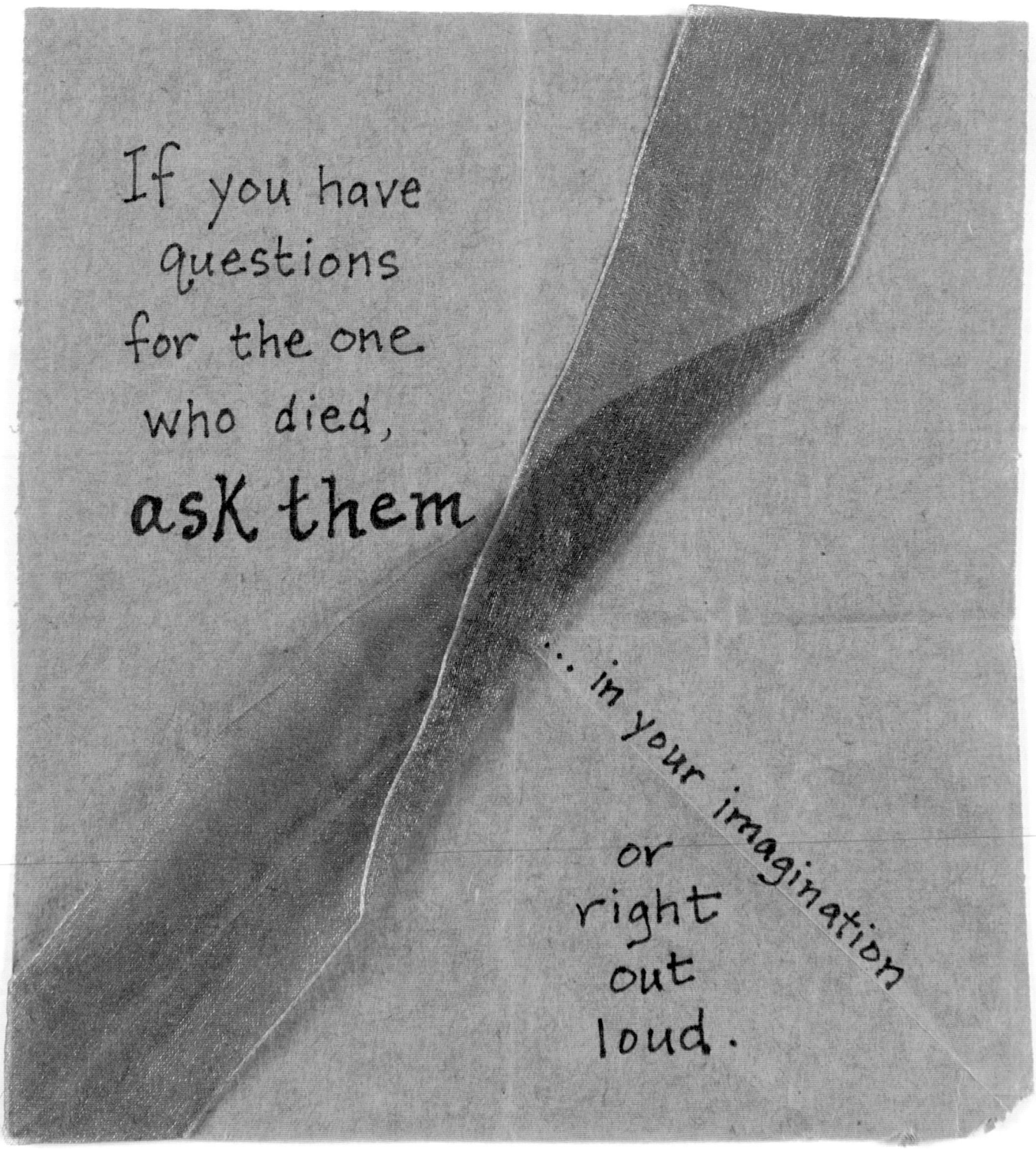
If you have
questions
for the one
who died,
ask them
... in your imagination
or
right
out
loud.

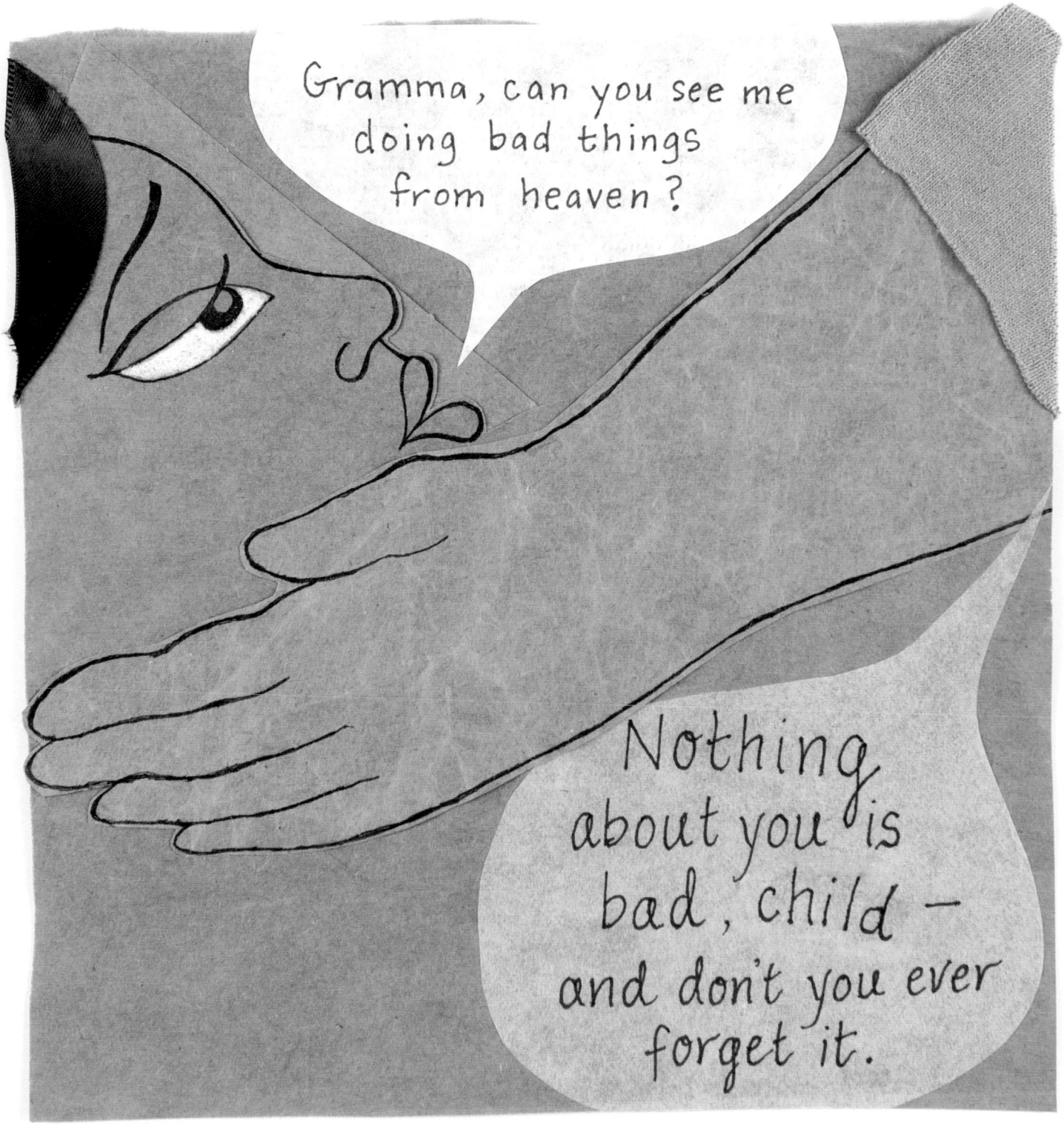
Gramma, can you see me doing bad things from heaven?
Nothing about you is bad, child – and don't you ever forget it.

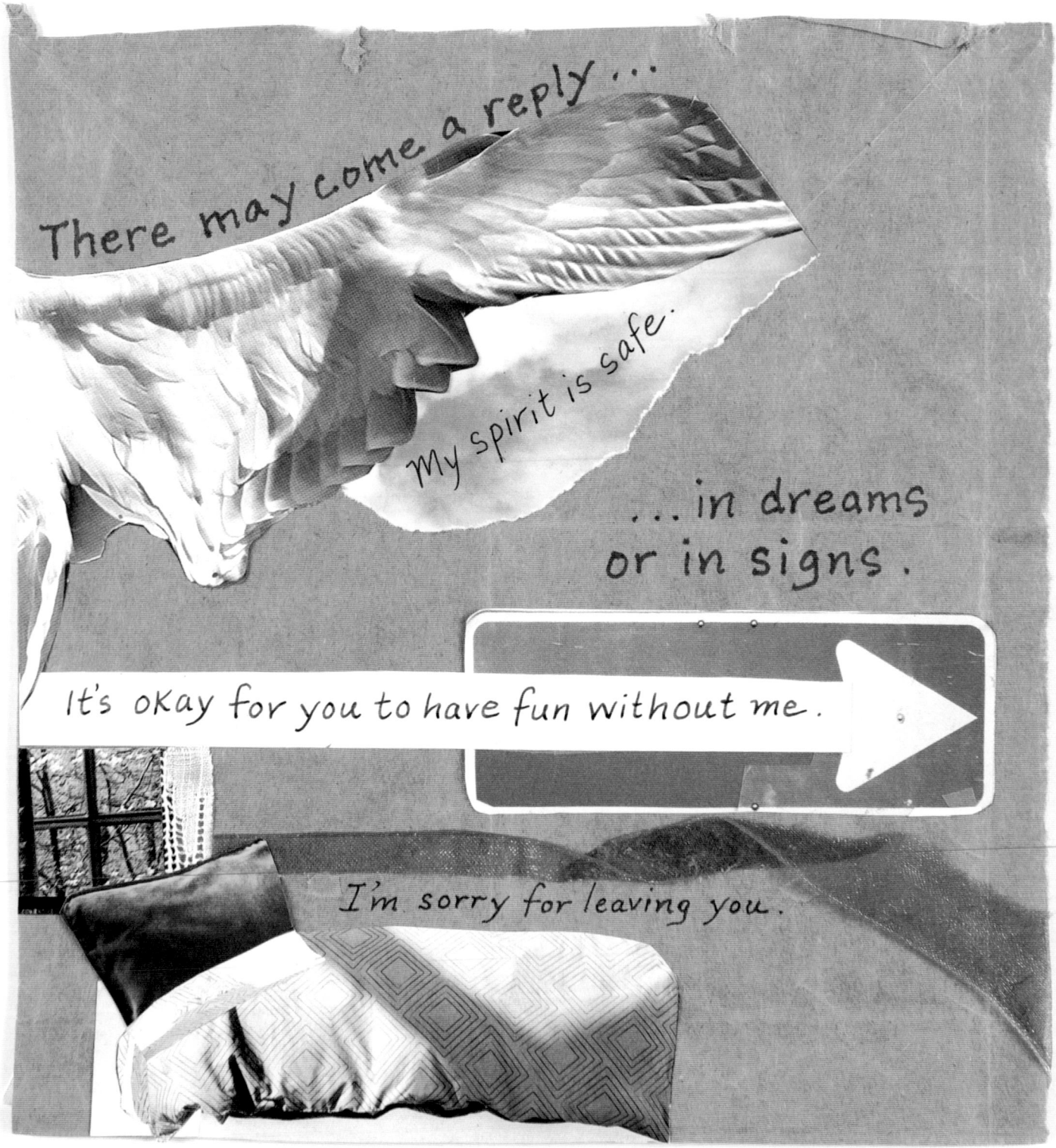
There may come a reply...
My spirit is safe.
...in dreams
or in signs.
It's okay for you to have fun without me.
I'm sorry for leaving you.

Where did she go?
Why do we have to die?

Gramma's garden is weedy, Dad.
It sure is.
She'd be so annoyed.
She would.
We don't get to Keep everyone we love who has ever lived.

Let's get you dressed.
But we do get to remember them

long after their lives
have ended.

Gramma died but her plants are alive.
Remembering lasts.

My mother fed and watered
everything out here —
including you and me..

Keep your connections to those who have died and to those still living.
Dad...

Would you teach me to make the sauce she made — in the boiling hot jars?
It would be an honor.
SIRI AN
CLACKAMAS
PRODUCE

These connections
make death
less scary
and they make
life more fun.
stupid

the end

Wanna know how to keep someone and, at the same time, let them go?

Wear
what they wore.
Play
what they played.
I'm in!

Read
what they read.
Hey! My name is in here!
Prayer Book
Whooooo wants some?
Make
what they made.
Me!
Yum!
Oooh me!
Me too!
Me!

Treasure
what was dear to them.
YOU

When an animal you care about dies, people may not understand your feelings.
FEEL THEM ANYWAY
We'll get another one.
What's the big deal?
It was only a _____.
animal you cared about
You're still sad about that?
Let me be.
Shield yourself from words that hurt you.

Here
is a place for the name or picture of
an animal
or maybe more than 1
whom you will remember always
Hey. You can hold a ceremony for a pet! Play a song. Plant a plant.
Say their name.

Names are magical.
They are like spells.
NONNO
Think of the name of the one you love who has died.
Picture it in ribbons, in sequins, in paper, in string.
MAMIE
Silver pen.
Gold pen.
Googly eyes.
Crayon.

Notice how it feels to
see it
hear it
say it
make it
Connie
Bo Dean
KATHY
Jidu
BRIT
Ethel Lee
Sandra
George + Anita

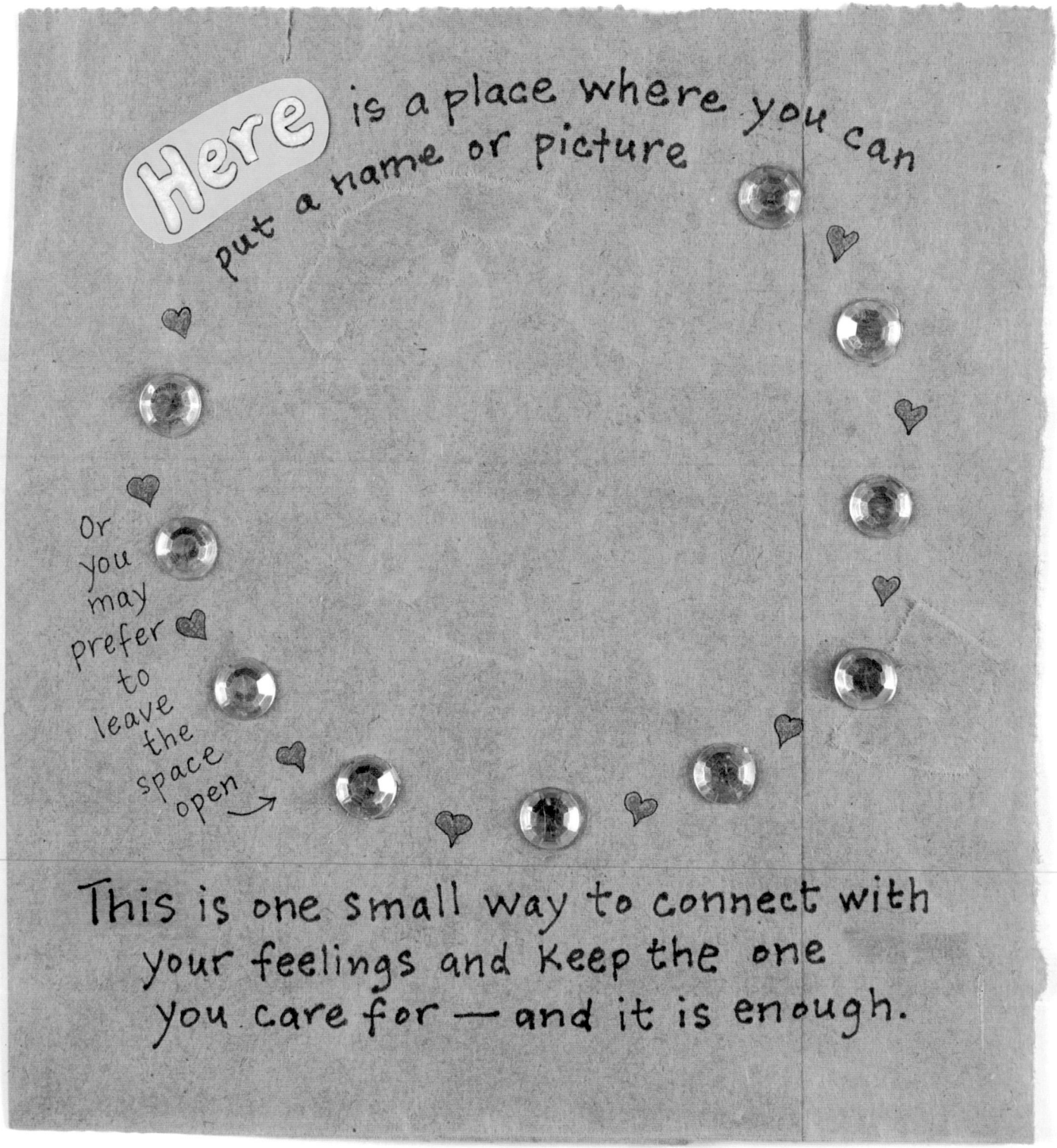
Here is a place where you can put a name or picture
Or you may prefer to leave the space open
This is one small way to connect with your feelings and keep the one you care for — and it is enough.

Anastasia Higginbotham's books about ordinary, terrible things tell stories of children who navigate trouble with their senses sharp and souls intact.

Help may come from family, counselors, teachers, and dreams — but it's the children who find their own way through.

Anastasia has been making books by hand her whole life as a way to cope with change and grow.

YOU CAN TOO!

ordinary
terrible
things
ordinary
terrible
things